DEW OF BENGAL WINTER

POETRY ON BENGAL'S WINTER SEASON !

ABHISHEK SENGUPTA

Xpress Publishing
An imprint of Notion Press

XpressPublishing
An imprint of Notion Press

Old No. 38, New No. 6
McNichols Road, Chetpet
Chennai - 600 031

First Published by Notion Press 2019
Copyright © Abhishek Sengupta 2019
All Rights Reserved.

ISBN 978-1-64678-522-3

Contents

Preface

In this book, I tried to describe wonderful winter season of Bengal. Bengal is a beautiful land. Full of greenery and life. Land of Bengal is one of the most fertile land in the world. Bengal sees all six seasons of India. But winter season has its own charm. It gives a respite from hot and humid summers.

With Autumn, the season starts cooling. It typically starts from arrival of Goddess of Autumn. Typically, this marks the end of rains and start of 10 days of Mega Carnival of Bengal, The Durga Puja. This season is identified by blooming of white coloured *"Kash"*flowers. Exact differentiation of seasons is quite difficult here, but local Bengalis can confidently can do so by studying Bengali calendar months.

Winter in Bengal calls for new rice and mouth-watering sweet items. New rice comes up and of course calls for festivity in countryside. Most important sweet, which worth mentioning is Jaggery. This is one of the best and most awaited item. Jaggery based sweets are a craze here. If you do not have a sweet tooth, you will develop one here. Aroma of sweets are fascinating.

Bengali calendar is predominantly lunar calendar. Full moon and no moon nights are celebrated nights here. I have mentioned full moon nights many places during composition. Full moon during winter is quite wonderful, especially when you see it on lake waters.

Chillness of Bengal comes from flow of northerly winds. I have mentioned this many times in this book. This makes the winter, a lazy season.

Winter flowers of Bengal are quite beautiful. One must see the variety of flowers that grows in winter. I have described one here in this book.

Best of all, dew on the grass, during winter, is an instrument of outburst of emotion for Bengalis.

I wish you all a happy reading !
Abhishek Sengupta
Author

1. Winter Come Like Some

With festivity go up & dew comes down,
Sky comes on with deep, deep down,
Deep clouds get sight with low light,
Day get on more and more bright,
Night brings dew to lines of grass,
Calmness of dark bring the jazz,
Day light takes time to come
That's when the winter come like some.

Scorching sun turn to pleasant warm,
Rains in its way closes its term,
Pleasantness of weather is the mood,
Sun smiles with the face full stood,
Northerly breeze chills the bone,
Night makes dew cover the stone,
Quite night refreshes the soul like mum,
That's when the winter come like some.

Morning gets song of vendors' ferry,
Faint light of sun make the merry,
Fog makes us pleasant like mystery,
All the remains get part of history,

Milkmen gets to sing while on rolls,
Memory of winter sticks like gum,
That's when the winter come like some.

• 2 •

Brightness of garden flower makes colour,
All beauty takes its toll like winter chiller,
Scent of flower take way to heart,
All refreshes the mood like thousand watt,
Beauty of way comes to great green,
Bengal's nature remains well seen,
Nature makes all heart and soul numb,
That's when the winter come like some.

2. Winter Season

Breeze of North hits the weather,
Leaves of tree go on shredder,
Dew of grass make the morning wet,
Golden light of sun make the story set,
Light breeze of morning makes the bone chill,
People do like the wonderful winter feel,
No lazy beds can discard sweet reason,
Chill & shine make the great winter season.

Rays of sun go weak like fall of leaves,
New rice makes its way sweet smell reaps,
Sweets of Bengal, makes the way,
Jaggery, much awaited, makes the say,
Aroma of sweetness take the toll,
Satisfies & smile, touches soul,
All day makes us more, less on,
Chill & Shine make the great winter season.

Season of harvest, of new rice takes on,
Rice of fine quality goes head on,
Quick and short showers really peeps,
Dew and fog, goes on for sweeps,
Land gets ready for more and more,

Crops get on, ready for next sore,
Awaited season moves for through joy fission,
Chill & Shine make the great winter season

• 4 •

Fog of morning makes wonderful feel,
Land makes totally crops, harvest & steel,
Winter holidays & Christmas make the air,
New year & celebration makes all fair,
"Poush" and holy dip makes soul great,
Waves takes away all worries though straight,
Soul & goodness make the man of clear vision,
Chill & shine make the great winter season.

3. Morning Calm Say

Night dark recedes,
Morning light seeds,
Mist of winter takes,
All then wakes,
Golden light takes the way,
"Hi"! is what the morning calm say.

Everyday comes,
Chillness takes warm,
Soft sounds of birds,
Speak million words,
Wake up O! Man get on you may,
"Hi"! is what morning calm say.

Green grass greet dew,
Greatness will know few,
Morning flower takes on,
Wrote from garden to lawn,
Get On, come out of stay,
"Hi" ! is what morning calm say.

Mild breeze touches,
Northerly all watches,

Chill touches the heart,
Takes way on the cart,
Day waiting for you, don't make it grey,
"Hi"! is what morning calm say.

Water on lake waves,
Mankind it saves,
Greetings comes from white swan,
Goes like this for everyone,
Day is all for you O! Great don't lay,
"Hi"! is what morning calm say.

4. Mist Of Morning

Winter sun takes the way,
Dew filled grass path, on the lawn of nature way,
Mist of morning there to Say Hi !

Fog of the dawn takes the leap,
Ray of golden light touches the earth like whip,
Mist of morning there to say Hi !

Pins people to drop like lazy,
Blanket cover of man fakes on winter crazy,
Mist of morning there to say Hi !

Chill feel of seasons northerly breeze,
Winter flower holds colourful bind it for freezing
Mist of morning there to say Hi !

5. Night flowering Jasmine

On morning of mist,
I walked to countryside of Bengal to see nature's wrist,
Got mesmerized by night flowering jasmine.

With dew on grass,
While flower of heaven drop but in royal way in mass,
Got mesmerized by night flowering jasmine.

Greatest beauty of nature,
White and orange of flora is the best of all God's creature,
Got mesmerized by night flowering jasmine.

Mother nature's best gift,
Arrives with Goddess of Autumn, falls in morning with great
swift,
Got mesmerized by night flowering jasmine.

Flower of paradise,
Comes with Goddess of strength, wealth and destruction,
with great rise,
Got mesmerized by night flowering jasmine.

Festivals on roll with divine flower,

Covers ground draws like heavenly matter, all as flower
shower,
Got mesmerized by night flowering jasmine.

•

With outbreak of dawn,
Bring greatness & beauty of God's heaven to earth on the
lawn,
Got mesmerized by night flowering jasmine.

Mix of flora and dew,
Morning fog on the way, mix of Bengal mist with chants, its
few,
Got mesmerized by night flowering jasmine.

6. Winter's Full Moon

Chillness of night,
Takes on the sky with full moon's sparkling might,
On the dark, taking off darkness,
Winter's full moon is Bengal's marquees !

Stillness of night,
Hold on the way, to the lanes and by lanes right,
Greenery takes on moonlight harness,
Winter's full moon is Bengal's marquees !

Calmness of night,
Takes the land to pond to see the sky white,
Noir takes on the land's sharpness,
Winter's full moon is Bengal's marquees !

Seriousness of night,
Sky busting with glitters and spreading light,
Quietness of dark says a lot harmless
Winter's full moon is Bengal's marquees !

Witness of night,
Brightness of great land under moon, great sight,
Great time takes place's greatness,

Winter's full moon is Bengal's marquees !
Shrillness of night
Walks on the standing paddy fields to make it bright
Fine time take on everyone's illness,
Winter's full moon is Bengal's marquees !

Massiveness of night
Grass and dew, takes the ground with amazing fight
Nature takes up its amazing circus,
Winter's full moon is Bengal's marquees !

Willingness of night,
Best time of day to feel nature to see great height,
Mother nature is there to beat all smart chase,
Winter's full moon is Bengal's marquees !

7. Winter Night

On the stillness of the night,
With moon at sky, surrounded by twinkling star fight,
I sit on side on winter night.

Silence prevails around,
Day's run finally ends with all way to stop all sound
I feel the vacuum on winter night.

Mild blow of northerly,
Hits the skin with hard icy feel, in its own feel of motherly,
I stay on way on winter night.

Moonlight brightens countryside,
Bengal's hut, waterbodies & lanes makes the vision wide,
I stare all the way on winter night.

Green grass tip of dew
Moonlight makes it diamond tip on nature's best few,
I get surprized on winter night.

Sudden sound of bird,
Confused with bright moon as its way to out of word
I heard all on winter night.

Combing paddy field,
Makes land rich with its own crop full of prosperity & yield
I joy out on the winter night.

Flow from north,
Break, firm image of moon on lake, makes it take worth,
I shiver on the winter night.

Sudden crack of bicycle bell,
Reminds, how hard son of land makes to fill the tail,
I wonder on the winter night.

Sleeps the world of all,
Night rolls on and on, deep and chill to its fall
I realize on the winter night.

8. Best Month

Knock of winter,
With breeze of cold in its own, and December as its splinter,
Best month is here !

Pleasant day on,
Touch of mist on the way, today with dew on lawn,
Best month is here !

Golden Sun fades fog,
Flower of winter rolls the way on bird's sound rock,
Best month is here !

Dew on grass,
Flocking of fauna with south movement of birds,
Best month is here !

Shiver of northerly wind
Takes the great mood out of mind, pleasures pinned
Best month is here !

Touch of cold,
On the winter dawn like best to be in bed-fold
Best month is here !

Sign of relief
Like way off the way in chills day of falling leaf,
Best month is here !

Morning blues on
The complete season says "Hi" at dawn
Best month is here !

Time on & gone
So enjoy Bengal's sweet & jaggery and keep on,
Best month is here !

9. Winter Rain

With northerly hit,
Bengal takes a leap to chill of season in its own lit,
Drizzles run down with winter rain !

Chill of north,
Hits the east to fill the heart with warmth, it worth,
Drizzles run down with winter rain !

Morning gets blue,
People in plain enjoys season with awesome clue,
Drizzles run down with winter rain !

Jackets on with,
Seasons takes on, takes the sun on sheds, warm in a myth,
Drizzles run down with winter rain !

Dawn gets on,
Dimmed and diffused light takes on with clouds born,
Drizzles run down with winter rain !

Jaggery flow,
With temperature going down sweet of season starts glow,
Drizzles run down with winter rain !

Sweets of land,
Flow of taste takes leap to best of taste, its stand,
Drizzles run down with winter rain !

Touch of fog,
With drops of sky its own way to take nature's log,
Drizzles run down with winter rain !

Farms of east,
Get ready for the amazing crop yield to final feast,
Drizzles run down with winter rain !

Touch of rain & wind,
Makes Bengal land winter green with amazing kind,
Drizzles run down with winter rain !

10. O ! Winter

Grasses grace in cold,
Best of season to say as told,
Great time here to see and feel as it enter,
You are here O! Winter.

Calm of dawn,
Watch of nature, flower of day in lawn,
Touch of season, goes as and on to bitter,
You are here O! Winter.

Mild shrill of bird,
Breaks the silence of calm until heard,
Makes nature, nurture best of way like her,
You are here O! Winter.

Time of Day,
Goes the time in the rhyme of say,
Chill of north takes the route and it linger,
You are here O! Winter.

Weak sun peeps,
Soft soul gets up in freeze as it weeps,
Day moves on with great way like splinter,

You are here O! Winter.

Day rolls on,
Dusk takes the way with its gone,
Chill gets back with dark as the sky starts glitter,
You are here O! Winter.

Breeze of north,
Takes the day's warmth and its worth,
Fall of cold to the dark time, for getting silver,
You are here O! Winter.

Clear sky,
With moon on zenith, stars go shy,
Whole of night gets blanket of dark like canvas for painter,
You are here O! Winter.

11. O! Winter Night

Stillness follow the path
Bright moon gives Bengal land light bath,
Time to see shade & light
Its chilly O! Winter Night

Green with dew,
Great scene to see the way it matches few,
Darkness stand the way like knight
Its Chilly O! Winter night.

Appearance of fog,
Wood gets moist with touch of drop on log,
All take the day way right,
Its Chilly O! Winter Night.

Water of lake
Broken moon image sets the stage,
Nature may make after daylight,
Its Chilly O! Winter night.

Mistakenly birds wake,
Its moonlight, not sun, for God's sake,
Full-grown crops turn white

Its Chilly O! Winter night

Fall of chill,
Makes environment, its way and still
Takes the way lazy inspite
Its Chilly, O ! Winter night.

Flow of feed,
Bengal fertile & ready for the winter seed
Sweet tooth takes the bite
Its chilly O! Winter night.

Land of warmth like,
Turn to bitter winter finally strike
Hits heard with frosty might
Its Chilly O ! Winter night.

12. Kolkata's Misty Morning

Morning Chill takes the way,
To awesome greenery of Bengal say,
Dew on grass nature's learning,
That's Kolkata's misty morning !

Soft sun takes slow crawl,
Sellers get off train for daily brawl,
Rails on roads takes trams to turning,
That's Kolkata's misty morning !

Newspaper takes on eyes,
Morning walkers take piping tea are ties,
Horn of vehicle throws nature warning,
That's Kolkata's misty morning !

Winters flower boom on,
Migratory birds makes home the lawn,
Cool northerly comes like storming,
That's Kolkata's misty morning !

Street dogs retires to coil,
Dew of grass takes on to the wet soil,

Holders of Bengal's fertile land takes to farming,
That's Kolkata's misty morning !

Shrillness of morning local train,
Sweeps on to the silent lane,
Street takes look on wonders pouring,
That's Kolkata's misty morning!

13. Winter Drink

When earth calm with full chill,
Heart take son with own feel,
Time to feel the way too sink,
On hand glass full of winter drink !

Fall of dusk to the dead of dark,
On the way to see the silence mark,
Time to go and wander to soul's link,
On hand glass full of winter drink !

Sip takes the soul to get off the day's
To feel the inner path that passes off way's
One of way moves of dark from pink,
On hand glass full of winter drink !

Heart's inner core comes out,
Belief of way takes picture stout,
Your heart's canvas is blank, all yours' to ink,
On hand glass full of winter drink!

Glass takes on the road of emotion,
See on the path to take on life's station,
Feeling flows, as metal from gold to zinc,

On hand glass full of winter drink!

Glass goes on, takes on steps as on,
All anxiety takes over by glass, now gone,
Inner peace flows on, with eye's blink,
On hand glass full of winter drink!

14. Bells Jingle

Winter hitting Kolkata with bells,
All the wonder of stress down wells,
Eve of Christmas goes up on high,
Lights of Park Street goes on sky,
Way out full on festivity with light,
Food, Sizzlers, wine, foodie turns bright,
Children, oldies, students, men & girls with bangle
All are out, the bells jingle.

Strokes of midnight bell starts on,
All differences go too far, gone,
Churches, Cathedrals are all full,
Prayers, masses nothing on dull,
Santa caps on, with smile fun,
All ages go for the way on run,
Barriers fade, lights on, all goes mingle,
All are out, the bells jingle.

Bands are on, will go till down,
Grills & smoke, aromas go warn,
Drinks and wine takes full toast on,
Turkey on plate, people at restaurant or lawn,
Tons of roamers out on eve of Jesus,

All on move, on lights and up on wises,
Youngster go for, all eve of single,
All are out, the bells jingle.

• 27 •

15. Winter Breeze

On the shiny night,
On the calm way of the moon's white,
On December night freeze,
With the flow of winter breeze!

Touch of way on the sight,
Fall of say to its way of night,
Fog on the front when the beats seize,
With the flow of winter breeze!

Calm on the way on where,
Silence of the Bengal night on stare,
Northerly takes life to its lease,
With the flow of winter breeze!

Combing the paddy on the field,
Takes the life on total shield,
Winds and moon are on total tease,
With the flow of winter breeze!

Waves of the water in lake,
On the silence and calm feels like fake,
Life coils with wonders of winter freeze,
With the flow of winter breeze!

16. Melody Voice

Dawn of winter makes all shine with smile
Scorching heat goes out & get off for while,
With fog getting off, with dew pulling on,
Green grass makes on through quite lawn,
Mid of which, person keeps paddling his rickshaw,
With sweet humming voice, cold go for thaw,
With calm of dawn and melody of choice,
Mid of all, he keeps on with melody voice.

Paddle keeps on, amid great morning calm,
Clarity of wind with cold keep like balm,
Winter flower keep greet the voice of song,
Mild breeze with voice make the way long,
Van takes the turn of road, going still,
Calm of morning going on with its own chill,
Still of calm, scratches with mild noise,
Mid of all, he keeps on with melody voice.

Scent of morning flower greets the man,
Purity of dew, pours on from the can,
Paddle rolls, vans goes, piercing through Bengal wood,
Mild morning mist, nature greets, she could,
Gentle greet of smile by village girls flock,

Pebble crack below his van with soft knock,
Nothing can break rhythm of his Joyce,
Mid of all, he keeps on with melody voice.

Slant and weak rays of sun, spreads soft warm
Ponds of Bengal, flickers the giant swarm,
Lotus boom, with dew filled hibiscus,
Night flowering Jasmine scents goes like discus,
Van goes on with turn by paddle with on,
Blooming marigold on dew filled lawn,
Greatness of tune goes on smiled by ongoing boys,
Mid of all, he keeps on with melody voice.

Van moves on goes through lanes by lanes,
Releases all the way and passes all tense,
Takes toll on soul, goes on and on,
Touches all heart takes a great ton,
Passes on and on and on like its own,
Rhythm stays right, so is his tone,
Sweetness of his voice goes like toys,
Mid of all, he keeps on with melody voice.

17. Northerly Way

On the winter night,
When chill blocks the sight,
All prefer inside stay,
On flow of northerly way !

Winter moon strays,
Crops comb the field graze,
All sleeps they say,
On flow of northerly way !

Grass tops the dew,
Steps makes few,
Breeze fully lay,
On flow of northerly way !

Silence takes on,
Heaviness of soul makes on,
Its the season, it may,
On flow of northerly way !

Flow touches bone,
Takes soul to inner lone,
Night hits hard after soft day,
On flow of northerly way !

18. Winter Freeze

Time of winter,
Chill of best seasons splinter,
Flow of breeze,
Makes winter freeze !

Clear sky blue,
Dew of grass takes clue,
Soul goes cease,
Makes winter freeze !

Best month of year,
Awesome time to gear,
Takes this time on lease,
Makes winter freeze !

Morning mist,
Makes nights wonderful feast,
Dawn makes nature tease,
Makes winter freeze !

Evening dusk,
Fall of day end to wonderful husk,
We blend to thank on knees,
Makes winter freeze !

19. Winter All the Way

Mercury take a fall,
This makes proud spirit stand high and tall,
Feel the nature, they say,
Winter all the way !

Ray of sun gets slant,
Scorching sun takes a turn as it goes blunt,
Stand and move as its way,
Winter all the way !

Morning mist now takes,
Chill fill all the right as the day it makes,
Nature spread goodness, it lay,
Winter all the way !

Northerly flows down,
From Hills of north in its route to see crop brown,
Nature takes it on stay,
Winter all the way !

Grass bathe with dew,
Takes feel way to heart on the road it few,
Makes one's heart blue and grey,

Winter all the way !

,

Time rolls on,
So is the day, moves dusk from the start of dawn,
One sees spirit of heart all the day,
Winter all the way !

Rise of red sun,
To flow of breeze to the wonders of heart like fun,
Steals heart like, sun takes on hay,
Winter all the way !

20. Return Of Chill

Arrival of chill sudden,
When all thought of hike in heat as burden,
Back of northerly winds take fill,
Return of Chill !

Way of flow,
Northerly makes the mercury slow,
Cold takes the steal,
Return of Chill !

Change of flash,
Makes on the way will cold lash,
It takes way to feel,
Return of Chill !

Season of jiggery goes on,
New crops makes Bengal new lawn,
New cuisine fills meal,
Return of Chill !

Northerly takes flow,
Takes the spirit high and nature low,
Rolls on like reel,

Return of Chill !

Enjoy the slant sun,
Makes the environment full of fun,
Mother Nature sighs deal,
Return of Chill !

A Thank You !

I take this oppurtunity to thank all readers for reading my composition. In this book I tried to present a beautiful picture of Bengal's winter season. This is also season of celebration and festivity. I have not gone much into festivity. Festivity you will find in my next upcoming book.

I hope you have enjoyed the book. Please write me with your feedback and suggesstion at abhisheksengupta2006@gmail.com

Thanks and regards

Abhishek Sengupta